THE MOMMY BREAK PROJECT
A SELF-CARE MANIFESTO

THE MOMMY BREAK PROJECT
A Self-Care Manifesto

NICOLE WALKER

To my husband Roy, who enabled me to have a "mommy break project", I love you!

First Printing: 2018

ISBN 978-0-359-07770-0

www.themommybreakproject.com

THE MOMMY BREAK PROJECT

CONTENTS

INTRODUCTION 9

"HELLO, NICOLE! IT'S NICE TO MEET YOU AGAIN" 11

I GOT AN "S" ON MY CHEST.......................................21

I THINK I LOVE MY KIDS...27

MOMMY GUILT IS REAL... THEN IT GOES AWAY 33

MOMMY BREAK BY ANY MEANS NECESSARY.....................39

HOW I MADE IT HAPPEN AND HOW YOU CAN, TOO!...........45

MY YEAR OF MOMMY BREAKS...............................49

NOW, IT'S YOUR TURN...65

A LETTER FROM THE *OLD* ME TO THE *RE-FOUND* ME 71

THE MOMMY BREAK PROJECT

INTRODUCTION

Mommy breaks are imperative to the physical, mental, and emotional health of moms. Without them, we will not have the long-term mental, physical, and emotional stamina to successfully make it through this thing called motherhood. This is now your manifesto. **Read this. Embrace this. Own this.**

Mommy breaks are designed to inspire you to take action, to be intentional about your self-care. Your partner will thank you. Even your kids will thank you one day, too. If you begin to prioritize yourself as much as you prioritize everyone else, one day you will look back at this moment as a new beginning and you will surely look in the mirror and say, "Thank you."

THE MOMMY BREAK PROJECT

1

"Hello, Nicole!
It's Nice to Meet You Again."

You know, I was a happy and thriving young woman before I had children. Let me take you back to my mid-20s. In spring 2004, I had just moved to the big city of Chicago from Ann Arbor, Michigan, where I graduated with my master's degree. I was excited to relocate, to start the "post-college student" chapter of my life. I was meeting new people and establishing my roots!

Along with the move to a new city, came the purchase of my first home. It was a condo in a gentrifying neighborhood that left a lot to be desired for me and my parents. The silver lining was a really cute guy who bought a condo across the street from me four months after I moved in. We would eventually meet at a housewarming party in his building and disrupt my grandiose dreams of having a fun, innocent dating life and meeting lots of new people. God must have had other plans. Our friendship quickly blossomed into a romantic relationship. We both acknowledged that we were "geographically undesirable" because we were in such close proximity and it would be disastrous if we broke up. Even after falling in love, I stayed busy by volunteering, pursuing my passions, and going to different events around the city. I was having a great time. If I could describe "Nicole before kids," I would be described as a knitting, entertaining, chick-lit reading, entrepreneurial loving, traveling, altruistic, wannabe triathlete, and a foodie. Doesn't she sound pretty dope? I think so, too!

Fast-forward five years later. I have two years under my belt as a "wife," which is a title I am still trying to figure out, and I am in the hospital enduring a 30-hour labor. After experiencing a labor injury, I had the "pleasure" of having an equally stressed mother in the delivery room as I tried to figure out how to nurse my beautiful, screaming newborn daughter. I ALWAYS knew that I wanted to have children, but my delivery experience set the tone for how I would feel through my first year and a half as a mother—overwhelmed and exhausted. I cried after my mom's two-week stay ended. She was leaving me with a human being that came with no instructions; someone who wanted to nurse constantly. HELP! Moms, did you experience similar feelings?

Right when I felt like I found my groove, I got pregnant again. In fact, my second child was conceived the weekend of my daughter's birthday. How do I remember, you ask? Because, as I am sure any new mom can attest to: there was not a whole lot going on in the intimacy department, so I remembered every time. My son was born nine months later. Another beautiful nine-pound baby, but this time I felt like, "I got this...I know what to expect."

Fast-forward 18 months later and I had two kids under two years old. Neither were potty-trained. Sleep was a distant memory. My husband and I felt like we were being hazed. I was overwhelmed, exhausted, and felt like I was epically failing as a mother. The concept of "self-care" was foreign to me. Was it just me as a new mom that it was foreign to?

Although I enjoyed occasionally hanging out with my friends and having spa treatments on my birthday, self-care was not a priority. During the baby and young toddler stage, I yearned for an evening of uninterrupted sleep more than retail therapy or a manicure. It was as if someone took the air out of me. It's the type of exhaustion that most new moms can relate to.

I struggled to find my new normal. I was exhausted all the time. I wondered if I was doing the right things to raise my children to be perfect. My only saving graces were a hands-on husband, girlfriends who were already moms who normalized motherhood, and a home daycare provider who constantly reassured me that I was not going to lose my mind! Between trying to embrace my post-baby physique, work a full-time job, maintain a clean house, and (oh, yeah!) be a "good wife," I often wondered if I would always feel so tired and disorganized.

Although I was still trying to find my way in motherhood, my entrepreneurial spirit remained relentless. When my oldest child turned two, I applied to a startup incubator with the goal of creating an app that curated dating experiences. Who joins a startup incubator with two babies at home? I did, and the timing was horrible.

I was exhausted, but I was not a quitter. Over the next two years, I pivoted away from a dating app and started brainstorming and making many failed attempts to determine ways to engage moms around the idea of making time for ourselves. As supportive as my friends were, I also learned that I could not build a business counting on their consistency.

After a few months of fun, but low-attended events, I decided to turn the attention to myself. This is how the "Mommy Break Project" was born. It was a win-win. I would rediscover the things I enjoyed doing, blog about them, and recommit to being intentional about my life by first being intentional about the way I took care of myself.

When I first mentioned my goal to chronicle my journey of taking a mommy break at least once a week for a year, one friend said that it would be impossible. My husband may not have been passionate about my goal either, but like all of my entrepreneurial endeavors, he was very supportive. Why did a commitment to regular self-care sound like such a huge feat among my friends? The growing skepticism from those around me made the challenge all the more appealing. I was going to make the impossible feel possible.

Once you become a mom, you will always be a mom. Barring no tragedies, this badge of honor that is bestowed upon us is a journey. It is a journey of ups and downs. It is a journey of different seasons. It is a journey filled with joys and maybe sadness when you start seeing your kids grow up. I know this to be true and I am only seven years in!

My time is always going to be shared with my kids whether we are at home together, when I am at work planning for them, or when we have those moments away from the hustle and bustle of life together on vacation. This is all the more reason why there was a need to create a new normal for our family, one that included making time for myself. To not prioritize myself, now sounds like signing up for a slow death of the Nicole I knew and loved.

This year focused on me has not been without its challenges, but it has truly been awesome! I am still always tired, overwhelmed at times, and not that confident in my "mommy walk." But in spite of these things, I have a moment of "me time" each week to look forward to. I will never return to the old normal of weeks and weeks passing without at least getting out for a manicure, martini, or massage with, or without, the companionship of my husband or girlfriend(s). Now, I want to share everything I learned on my journey with you.

Before beginning your mommy break journey, consider these things:

- It's hard to be intentional about your "me time." It's really hard. But it's worth the hard work to make it happen.

- Quality time with your spouse or partner qualifies as a mommy break. Your new focus should not result in your partner feeling neglected.

- The need to clean will always be present; don't allow household chores to keep you from your mommy break.

- There may be non-mommy friends who never invite you out because you are a mom now. Don't take it personally. There is no malicious intent in the lack of invitations from them. If they don't extend the invitation, you should!

- You will have mommy friends who are consumed by motherhood. Extend the invitation for them to join you on a mommy break, even if there is a high likelihood that they will say "no."

- The sky is not going to fall if I put myself first. It may feel like it in the moment, but it's oftentimes temporary. You will be mad at yourself for succumbing to the pressures of home.

- Mommy breaks can come in all shapes and sizes. "Me time" can exceed your expectations even on the simplest mommy breaks.

- Always try to end the week on your terms because you have no idea what tomorrow may bring.

- Don't feel guilty about fitting in two mommy breaks within one week. If the stars align, go for it.

- Don't underestimate your significant other/partner/ spouse. They do listen and know your heart more than we may give them credit for sometimes.

Mommy Break Key Takeaway #1

You were your own person before you were somebody's mom. Despite the never-ending exhaustion, it is worth rediscovering your passions and making the impossible desire of regular self-care a reality.

Let's Reflect

What would the "pre-mommy" you wish you would have never given up since becoming a mom?

THE MOMMY BREAK PROJECT

2

I Got an "S" on My Chest

You didn't know? Mommies are domestic superheroes. Think about all of the balls you juggle in the air effortlessly. Well, it is not effortlessly. We just make it look that way. We're employee, employer, housekeeper, taxi driver, personal chef, counselor, disciplinarian, companion, and lover. All in a day's work, right? When you give birth to a child, your brain becomes rewired to be a multitasking ninja. No matter how exhausted we may feel, we push through to ensure our family or household, does not fall apart. While I am blessed to have a husband who does his fair share, that does not alleviate the burden that I, and so many other moms, feel to stay on top of things.

Being a mom is the HARDEST job in the world. You are responsible for raising a human being to be a productive member of society. You are responsible for protecting them from harm's way. Supporting their emotional health. Nurturing their talents and gifts. Preventing them from being sugar addicts. Being strong when they feel weak. Encouraging them to eat their vegetables. Providing them with a safe and clean home. Regulating their screen time so that they don't become zombies. Cleaning up their puke and diarrhea. Kissing their snot-crusted cheeks even though you know you are probably going to get sick. Most importantly, loving them unconditionally and being their biggest cheerleader because life is hard.

And after you pour all of this into your children, you still have to be a wife, partner, significant other, daughter, friend, and employee. We, as moms, know how to dig deep and show up every day no matter how emotionally, physically, or mentally exhausted we are. And this is why we are superheroes! Even the days when we can only give 50 percent, it still looks like we are giving 100 percent to our families.

Even superheroes have epic fails like forgetting school spirit week, sending their kids to school without lunch, forgetting to wash your kids' swimsuits and sending them to a lesson with a dirty swimsuit instead. Don't judge me. If you don't already, you will have some examples soon. Trust me. We are still perfectly imperfect so have grace with yourself when your powers teeter out from time to time.

Beware! Figuratively speaking, every superhero has his/her kryptonite. For me, it is not getting enough sleep and pushing myself past my limits. You know what I mean? Like when you create a schedule that is not humanly possible to accomplish? The days when you have multiple birthday parties and need to go grocery shopping, and you try to do all of it. The moments when we just don't want to let our kids down, even if it is ultimately to our detriment. That's a mommy for you.

You know what? Nothing restores your superpowers more than a mommy break. So proudly wear that "S" on your chest and do what you need to do to keep those superpowers replenished and activated.

Mommy Break Key Takeaway #2

You are a real-life superhero. Wear your cape proudly!

Let's Reflect

What is your mommy superpower that makes you the domestic superhero that you are?

3

I THINK I LOVE MY KIDS

I know, I know. I might sound a little harsh, but it's true. I thank God every day that He blessed me with the opportunity to be a mom to two beautiful children. I truly cannot imagine life without them. They are my world. I cannot imagine not being a mom.

The first time I questioned my love for my kids was when my daughter caught norovirus at daycare. Who knew diarrhea makes viruses go airborne and that the sh*t—no pun intended—can still be under your fingernails even when you wash your hands raw. My husband and I got so sick. I was so pissed. I mean, how could changing a diaper and cleaning up puke from a beautiful baby nearly leave me feeling like I was on my death bed? I know she didn't do it on purpose, but I was mad that she made me that sick. OK, I said it! I had never experienced anything like it. In time I got better, but also became a germaphobe in the process. From that stomach virus episode on, plastic gloves and masks are a permanent fixture under my bathroom sink and should be under yours, too.

Although I always wanted to be a mom and do love them with all of my heart, my kids get on my nerves pretty regularly.

Here are my "I Think I Love My Kids" triggers:

1. Whining ("USE YOUR WORDS!")

2. Stalling before going to bed

3. Having problems following directions

4. Getting dressed slowly or not at all

5. Fighting

6. Saying "I'm bored"

7. Having tantrums

8. Tattling on each other

9. Being rude to others and not using their home training, making me look crazy in public in front of friends, or even complete strangers

10. Having trouble cleaning up behind themselves and then complaining that their room is messy. Well, then do something about it!

I could probably think of others, but these are the ones that come to the top of my mind for my children. I often wonder how your own flesh and blood, someone so cute and lovable, could be so annoying sometimes. Did my sister and I get on our parent's nerves like this?

How did they manage it? Or is this just a result of bad parenting?

We all know the moms in our circles who always have the plastic smiles on their faces, doting on and bragging about their kids, constantly. Be wary. Those moms are possibly ticking time bombs who might explode any day now. Calling it like it is and admitting the days when your children make you question your love, is healthy for everyone involved. We are completely normal. Really, we are.

Outside of the daily triggers of trying my patience, I really do love my kids, but handling them can be exhausting. I had to realize that my kids having an active social life meant that I could not have any social life, but I reject that idea, and I hope you do, too! It's insane to believe that their social life should get preference over my own. It is not a necessity that they are in every activity or in every elite club. When I reflect on my own childhood, the days that brought me the most joy were hanging out on the block with my friends, hosting a lemonade stand with my sister, and riding our bikes up and down the street. Not my mom carting my sister and I around to a bunch of activities every weekend. Don't get me wrong, structured social activities for children are good. They just don't have to rule our lives.

We have to be mommy every day, at least until our kids are 18. Even then, most mothers will never fully turn "mommy mode" off. Kids are not socially aware enough to give you a sick day when you feel that tickle in your throat or a mental health hour when you have a bad day.

What I know for sure is that the ONLY way I can manage my triggers and not step in the landmines my children set for me every day, is to take regular mommy breaks. That is the only solution because our kids are not going to stop getting on our nerves. The only way I can continue to give my unconditional love and devotion is to step out of the house and away from them. Grocery shopping for a moment of peace and quiet just isn't enough. So, the next time your kids get on your nerves and you feel like you are about to lose it, take that as a signal that you need to schedule a manicure and pedicure AS SOON AS POSSIBLE.

Mommy Break Key Takeaway #3

Loving your kids unconditionally includes loving yourself enough to know that they are about to push you over the edge. Escape immediately!

Let's Reflect

Have you ever had an *I-think-I-love-my-child moment?* How do you manage your triggers?

4

MOMMY GUILT IS REAL... THEN IT GOES AWAY

Outside of mommy chores, lack of childcare, and general exhaustion, what is the other thing that often gets in the way of you taking a regular mommy break? Mommy guilt. You know that feeling when you are making a choice that does not put your kids first? That feeling that makes you think that putting yourself first is, by default, automatically causing your children emotional harm. That sinking feeling in your heart that will cause you to abort all plans in order to spend more time with your kids. The pit in the bottom of your stomach when you call home during a work trip and your kids are crying because they miss mommy.

Have you ever experienced any of these mommy-guilt scenarios?

- Going to happy hour versus coming home to make dinner and help with homework
- Not staying at the birthday party like the rest of the moms
- Missing a sports game
- Refusing to sign up to be a chaperone during a class field trip
- Traveling every week for work
- Making your kids go to after care versus being available to pick them up early

Ever notice how "good dads" may feel a little guilty if they can't spend quality time with their kids, but they usually proceed with their plans? Some dads feel no qualms about choosing happy hour over their kids or doing the Sunday football marathon at their favorite sports bar with friends. You know why? Because they know mommy got it.

The absence of "daddy guilt" allows them to have a freedom in decision making that moms don't often experience. They don't think about the impact that they are making by not choosing to have quality time with their kids. They don't consider how stopping by the gym—instead of grocery shopping—may cause a delay in dinner, which will ultimately delay bedtime and result in sleepy, grumpy kids the next morning. None of that enters their psyche. Only ours.

Moms, mommy guilt may be our cross to bear, but I promise that it can go away. Maybe not immediately, but it does go away. Reality check: Do you really think 10 years from now that your 6-year-old is going to say, "Mommy, because you took regular mommy breaks, I am not the teenager I could be?" I wish my children would. So, in those moments when you are feeling burnt out and need a minute to regroup, take a moment, or even an hour, to recharge. Your kids will not benefit from quality time with mommy if mommy is emotionally and mentally depleted.

Mommy Break Key Takeaway #4

Push through the mommy guilt.

Let's Reflect

What are you going to do to manage your mommy guilt?

5

MOMMY BREAK BY ANY MEANS NECESSARY

MOMMY BREAK BY ANY MEANS NECESSARY! Say it with me!

This is the mindset you need in order to make regular mommy breaks your new reality. Your emotional, physical, and mental health as a mom is contingent on your commitment to take a mommy break by any means necessary. Some days that will mean not washing a load of clothes. Some days that will mean going to bed with the house a mess. Sometimes that will mean pushing through the mommy guilt and choosing yourself over your children. Sometimes that may mean enjoying quality time by yourself for yourself without the companionship of your girlfriend or spouse. There will always be something else to do, but remember that it will also be there even when the mommy break is over. Seriously, the mommy chore list is not going anywhere, so you might as well enjoy life regardless of whether every chore is completed or not.

How do you begin to commit to a "mommy break by any means necessary" mindset? You start by forming a mommy break dream team. This team consists of individuals who enable you to take the time you need for yourself. It can include your "supportive" spouse or partner, but there are also other critical players that need to be on the team.

Here is my minimum, necessary dream-team roster:

- **Housekeeper:** How many times does a nasty house get in the way of having the mental freedom to leave? For me, it's way too often. How do you combat that and not feel like you have to deep clean every weekend? Get a housekeeper. Sounds fancy, but it doesn't have to be. Maybe you hire someone just to do your floors and bathrooms. Or maybe you hire someone to turn over the closets at the beginning of the season or do some dusting and clean out the refrigerator and oven. Whatever your heart's desire, but you should explore hiring someone to serve in this role.

- **Babysitter:** Childcare is the number one reason why moms cannot get away. I am not suggesting that every sitter is worthy of watching your precious cargo. I am, however, advocating for you to find someone you trust so you can get out of the house and get your nails done!

- **Mommy Friend:** As nice as it would be for all of us to have accessible, willing, and able-bodied grandparents or an on-call sitter/nanny, that is not always the case. Ask a fellow mommy friend willing to watch your kids for an hour or so while you take the mommy break. Just make sure you return the favor, sooner than later.

- **Supportive Partner:** Yes, your supportive partner is a critical part of the dream team. Once you get that person on board he (or she) will be supportive and can help you get all the pieces in place to enable you to unapologetically embrace your "mommy break by any means necessary" mindset. Share your plans as far in advance as you can so that they won't feel like their "me time" is not as important as yours.

- **Bonus! Personal Therapist:** All jokes aside. You may truly have some mental challenges around how to be intentional about your self-care. Do not feel any shame if you choose to engage a neutral professional resource. It may be beneficial to talk through those challenges with a therapist and create a path to feeling comfortable and taking a much-deserved mommy break.

You have to decide your statute of limitations on how long you can tolerate going without a mommy break. Some moms are so consumed by motherhood that they will go weeks, even months, without taking a moment for themselves. How is that working for you? Are you feeling rejuvenated and refreshed or exhausted and burned out? Don't hit a wall of physical and emotional burn out before you decide to make mommy breaks a priority.

If I ruled the world, all moms would have a mommy break at least once a week. Those may be lofty goals, but I spent a year doing just that. That may not be reasonable for everyone starting out, but I think once a month is a great start with the goal to build up to once a week within a few months. Does it matter how old your kids are? No. It may just take a little more willpower and intention if you are blessed with a newborn or a toddler.

Mommy breaks have to become a non-negotiable. For moms, they have to be viewed as important as food and shelter. Seriously, because if they are not prioritized with the other things that are critical to your livelihood, you will always prioritize over them. Think of it like you do the necessity for sleep. Get your mind right on the importance of regular mommy breaks and the rest will fall into place.

Mommy Break Key Takeaway #5

#MommyBreakByAnyMeansNecessary

Let's Reflect

What are the mental and physical barriers preventing you from adopting a #MommyBreakByAnyMeansNecessaryMindset?

6

HOW I MADE IT HAPPEN AND HOW YOU CAN, TOO!

Since I completed my goal of taking at least one mommy break a week for a year, I have a couple of ideas on how to take a mommy break. Despite my best efforts, for a majority of my mommy breaks, I only planned them a week in advance. It required me to pay attention to the events coming across my Facebook feed and keeping a running mental tally of the things I wanted to do, especially if an event was during a specific season. I planned minimal mommy breaks that would require me to get a sitter. I also avoided planning them during times when my husband would not want to leave the couch for football season. I am a perfectly imperfect mom, so there were some weeks where life would get in the way and days would pass without a mommy break. In those instances, I would take a look at the commitments for the weekend and see how I could fit in some "me time."

Companionship wasn't mandatory to my mommy breaks. It was nice when my husband or a girlfriend could join me, but I did not want another person to be a prerequisite to my mommy break. My philosophy is that if you can't have fun by yourself, you can't truly enjoy the company of others. No one else was accountable for my self-care but me, so I had to have the mental resolve to enjoy anything and everything by myself. If you are tiptoeing into "solo dates," try going to see a good chick flick. I promise, you won't even notice that you are by yourself.

It didn't take long before I began to anxiously anticipate each mommy break at the start of each week. Every time I hopped in an Uber or pulled out from my garage, I exhaled. Even if it was as short as an hour or as long as a weekend, I took a moment to get centered and leave the tantrums, silly argument with my spouse, or rough day at work behind. On the days I felt the most exhausted, I pushed through it. Going to my room and locking my bedroom door does not quite give me the type of mommy break I am looking for. If it works for you, GREAT! No matter the exhaustion level, my commitment to myself through my mommy breaks allowed me to come back home with a little more spring in my step.

Mommy Break Key Takeaway #6

It does not have to take a lot of effort to make a mommy break happen! They are worth the effort!

Let's Reflect

How many missed opportunities to take a mommy break have you recently experienced?

7

MY YEAR OF MOMMY BREAKS

The following list details how I spent my year of mommy breaks. Use it for inspiration as you start your own mommy break project! My favorite mommy breaks were the ones where I was getting on a plane to get transported out of "mommy-dom." I also loved the mommy breaks that allowed me to experience something new like pound fitness and pottery classes. I rediscovered my love for plays and that I absolutely do not go and enjoy them enough. From plays, to retail therapy, to spa services, I experienced it all, and there are still a ton of things I haven't gotten to do. I guess that means I have to keep going on this journey. I hope that you can join me!

Here is my yearlong recap of the mommy breaks I enjoyed:

Week #1 - Pound Class

Mommy Break Tip: Trying new fitness classes allows you to decompress, connect with other moms, and release the endorphins you need to conquer whatever is waiting for you when you return. Not sure how to find fun classes? Apps like *Class Pass* could be a good first step.

Week #2 - Visiting a Knitting Store and Getting a Manicure

Mommy Break Tip: All mommy breaks are not equal. Sometimes they can help you focus on getting something off of your personal to-do list and still bring you joy.

Week #3 - Retail Therapy at Nordstrom Rack

Mommy Break Tip: Don't leave your emergency flashers on when you are making a quick stop for retail therapy after grocery shopping. You are fast, but not that fast. (A lesson I learned the hard way. Smile.)

Week #4 - Happy Hour with Friends

Mommy Break Tip: Bring a girlfriend along for the experience when you need the company.

Week #5 – Took Work Trip to Nashville and Enjoyed Cinco de Mayo Margaritas

Mommy Break Tip: You're worth the trip even if it is a quick cocktail with a girlfriend before resuming business as usual.

Week #6 - Attending Speak Sistah Speak With Special Guest Valerie Jarrett and Dress Like a Mom Charity Event at Evereve

Mommy Break Tip: Intellectually stimulating mommy breaks are a good thing!

Week #7 – Girls Trip to Puerto Rico

Mommy Break Tip: Trips that have a balance of relaxation and adventure can satisfy everyone's pallet.

Week #8 - JP Morgan Corporate Challenge Race

Mommy Break Tip: Focus on completion, not perfection.

Week #9 - Bachelorette Party

Mommy Break Tip: Weddings, anniversaries, birthdays, and other milestones are easy mommy breaks. Be intentional about celebrating these milestones with friends and family because tomorrow is not promised.

Week #10 - The Prince Experience at the House of Blues

Mommy Break Tip: Date night qualifies as mommy breaks. Get to planning!

Week #11 - Helping a Friend Unpack Her House (with Wine)

Mommy Break Tip: Giving your time to help a friend can be mutually beneficial.

Week #12 – Seeing Common at Ravinia and Shopping for Flowers at Home Depot

Mommy Break Tip: Maximize in-home service providers. My daughter's hair braider had to babysit for us before and even though it was not the purpose of her visit, we maximized her time!

Week #13 - Planting Flowers and Attending a 70th Birthday Party

Mommy Break Tip: Find opportunities to entertain. They are hidden mommy breaks if you enjoy the company you are entertaining.

Week #14 - Lakefront Walk with Girlfriends and Lunch

Mommy Break Tip: Embrace your different circles of friends and be intentional about nurturing your friendships with quality time. Sounds like a great excuse for easy mommy breaks.

Week #15 – Had Solo Cocktails with Tacos and Attended Silver Room Block Party

Mommy Break Tip: Look for "instant mommy breaks" and rediscover your spontaneity. Don't be in a rush to get back home to return to mommy mode. It will be there!

Week #16 - Drinks with Coworkers and Dinner with a Girlfriend

Mommy Break Tip: Children are to mommy breaks what kryptonite is to Superman. Only make an exception once and, if your hand is forced, make sure you have a device handy that they can become consumed by. Yes, I will let my kids be digital zombies if it gives me a minute to have an adult conversation.

Week #17 - Activate Chicago Week

Mommy Break Tip: Encourage daddy to take his daddy breaks. They need them as well, and it creates an easier future exit strategy for you when you need to get out of the house. Trust me. It works!

Week #18 - Girls Trip Moving Outing and Stevie Wonder Listening Party at Promontory Week

Mommy Break Tip: Embrace a mommy staycation at home every once in a while. Wine, no children, and a great magazine or book can make for a great break.

Week #19–20 Year High School Reunion

Mommy Break Tip: If the grandparents need to watch the kids for an extended period of time, give them a helping hand with a list of favorite meals, snacks, and an activity idea or two.

Week #20 - Outdoor Movie Night - Movies at the Walkers'

Mommy Break Tip: No matter how tempting it may feel, purchase everything you need to host an event in the days prior. Don't play yourself with the "Oh, that can wait until tomorrow, because it will be a quick trip." #NOT

Week #21 – Jazzin' at the Shedd Aquarium and Out of Town Wedding in Cleveland

Mommy Break Tip: Don't ever second-guess your time away out loud.

Week #22 - Hosted a Wedding Party BBQ and Took Work Trip to Dallas

Mommy Break Tip: When traveling for work, reach out to your friends and acquaintances who live in that city to make sure you are making the most of your trip.

Week #23 - Outdoor Spin Class on the Beach and Wine on the Beach with Girlfriends

Mommy Break Tip: Plan your mommy breaks when your husband or partner already has some plans for the kids.

Week #24 - Volunteering with Perfect Cadence at the Nonprofit New Moms

Mommy Break Tip: Find a nonprofit whose mission really resonates with you and volunteer at least once a quarter or twice a year. The value of your time and talents can sometimes be far greater than any monetary donation.

Week #25 – "Say It Witcha Chest" Party

Mommy Break Tip: Let your hair down and dance like no one is watching!

Week #26 - Virtual Reality Spin Class at Cycmode

Mommy Break Tip: Start thinking about the mental barriers that get in the way of you taking mommy breaks. Write them down and brainstorm ways to remove them.

Week #27 - Bottomless Mimosa Brunch at Fremont with Friends

Mommy Break Tip: If you are hanging out with other parents, share a sitter. It takes the pressure off of finding two separate sitters, and you can split the expense.

Week #28 - Wine Riot Week

Mommy Break Tip: Find an event that you can look forward to and will not let anything get in the way of you enjoying it. You need one of those at least once a year.

Week #29 - Retail Therapy and Manicure, At Home Wine with Girlfriend

Mommy Break Tip: Post bedtime is a great time to activate a mommy break. Inviting a girlfriend over to catch up over wine (or tea) can sometimes be just as good as going out. You don't always have to defer to folding laundry and turning on DVR recordings.

Week #30 - Epic Burger and Baby Registry Set Up with Girlfriend

Mommy Break Tip: Find an activity for your mommy break that can help you get centered.

Week #31 - Randolph Street Market

Mommy Break Tip: Find your local antique or specialty market. It will be time well spent and you may discover a new find.

Week #32 - Wine Tasting with Mommy Bloggers and NPN Working Moms Speaking Event Featuring Heidi Stevens

Mommy Break Tip: Parenting groups offer low cost and sometimes free events that feature dynamic speakers that can have you leaving the event with a little more "pep" in your mommy step.

Week #33 - Birthday Dinner for Hubby at RPM Steak and Innovation Challenge Judge at IIT

Mommy Break Tip: Don't just take a day off from work just to celebrate a birthday or kick off a vacation. Random days off do the mind good.

Week #34 - Christmas Decoration Shopping

Mommy Break Tip: When taking a big trip to Disney World, still focus on getting the kids down as soon as possible, so you can decompress.

Week #35 - Favorite Things Party with Girlfriends Week

Mommy Break Tip: Hosting a girl's night out does not need to be a big production. Keep entertaining easy and simple so you don't burn yourself out and kill your motivation to host one in the future.

Week #36 - The One of a Kind Show at Merchandise Mart and Common and Erykah Badu Concert

Mommy Break Tip: Don't sacrifice warmth to be cute. I thought, "Yeah, in and out of the Uber both places. I don't need a real winter coat." Wrong. #mommyshouldknowbetter

Week #37 - 9th Anniversary: Art of Touch Class at Spa Space and Dinner at Topolobampo

Mommy Break Tip: Create a mommy break that is intentionally focused on reconnecting with your significant other. The returns will far outweigh the effort to coordinate it.

Week #38 - Drinks with Girlfriend at Ja Grill

Mommy Break Tip: Don't underestimate or under-indulge in water before, during, or after you enjoy some wine or cocktails. Mommies do not have time to feel groggy or slightly hung over the next morning because your kids are not going to have any grace with you and their Saturday morning demands.

Week #39 - Retail Therapy and Detroit Vegan Soul

Mommy Break Tip: Splurge and treat yourself to that one thing you have been wanting for a really long time. It's worth it.

Week #40 - Coffee Break at Starbucks, Spa Day at Spa Space, Cocktails and Retail Therapy

Mommy Break Tip: I know I have said it once, but you must do a marathon mommy break day every once in a while. The opportunity may be once in a blue moon, so take advantage!

Week #41 - Date Night Fitness Class

Mommy Break Tip: Working out is a mommy break when you can enjoy a fun fitness class with friends!

Week #42 - Drop-Off Birthday Party with Retail Therapy and Sweet Mandy B Cupcakes

Mommy Break Tip: Shop local whenever you can to truly discover unique finds and take your mommy break in a new neighborhood to discover different parts in your city.

Week #43 - Chicago Restaurant Week with Friends

Mommy Break Tip: Plan a family date night. No, it won't be a mommy break, but it will be an opportunity to get something done with your partner that you have been meaning to do while enjoying "quality time" with your family.

Week #44 – Mac N Cheese Production's Hand Picked Supper Club

Mommy Break Tip: Start training your kids to understand they won't be able to do everything they are invited to do and that they may have to choose one over the other. We, as moms, may be too hard-headed to follow our own advice. I know I am.

Week #45 - Birthday Spa Date with Girlfriend and Dinner at Le Colonial with Husband

Mommy Break Tip: Don't work on your birthday.

Week #46 - Birthday Fitness Parties

Mommy Break Tip: When you create a fitness routine that's not disruptive to the family routine, you minimize any resistance to getting out the house. Fitness routines should also not count as your primary mommy break. It's a necessity.

Week #47 - Wakanda Movie Outing Mommy Break

Mommy Break Tip: Take a moment to have a "dream weekend" and experience something that you may think is not in your realm of reality. Dreaming every once in a while is good for the soul.

Week #48 - Benefit Cosmetics "Make-upper"

Mommy Break Tip: A little makeup can completely change your mood. Take a moment and visit a makeup counter to get a little pick me up.

Week #49 - School Fundraiser and Work Trip to Dallas

Mommy Break Tip: Beware of mistaking parent volunteer opportunities for mommy breaks.

Week #50 - Breach Play and Girls Trip to Atlanta

Mommy Break Tip: Start working on a plan to repair the breach in your "me time."

Week #51 - Aerial Yoga Class and Birthday Dinner with Friends

Mommy Break Tip: Always keep your mommy friends informed of any new experiences you are going to try so that they have an opportunity to join you!

Week #52 - Pottery Class

Mommy Break Tip: Always have a mommy break planned after a trip with the kids. Notice, I didn't say vacation.

Mommy Break Key Takeaway

The options for mommy breaks are limitless! Have fun planning!!

Let's Reflect

What is the best mommy break you have ever taken? What made it so special? When are you going to try to recreate that mommy break?

8

NOW, IT'S YOUR TURN

So, moms, I have shared how I started taking regular mommy breaks, multiple reasons why you need to take regular mommy breaks, and the mindset you need to make it happen! Some of you may be thinking, "That's awesome for you, Nicole, but I have been so consumed by motherhood, I really don't know where to get started."

Complete these four steps to get going!

1. Share with two people that you want to start taking regular mommy breaks. No, your children do not count as one of the two people.
2. Think about the common barriers that often get in the way of taking a mommy break and brainstorm how you can remove at least one of them.
3. Brainstorm some easy mommy breaks that have low barriers to making it happen by next week. I recommend starting with something easy to do like getting a manicure and pedicure while out going grocery shopping. The easier the mommy breaks you do such as taking a coffee break, or retail therapy, the easier it will be to build up the confidence to take a mommy break that requires a little bit more planning and coordination.

4. Create Your M.A.P.!

Your M.A.P. (Mommy Break Action Plan) provides a to-do list of the things you need to consider to make that next self-care moment go off without a hitch. Consider me your virtual accountability partner, committed to helping you find joy in being intentional about your self-care! You really can take regular mommy breaks, but first you need a plan. Let's get to work!

MOMMY BREAK ACTION PLAN

What changes are you going to make today to enable yourself to take regular mommy breaks? For example, hire a sitter, create a mommy break/daddy break schedule with your partner, etc.

What are your favorite things to do?

What is your favorite day of the week to take a mommy break?

What is the best time of day for you to take a mommy break?

How frequently will you take a mommy break?

What will you do for your next mommy break?

Who will you invite to join you on your mommy break? (This is optional. I have a ton of fun by myself.)

What is the date for your next mommy break?

What is the date for the next three mommy breaks?

Next Steps:
- Tear out this mommy break action plan.
- Put your mommy break date on the family calendar.
- Implement you M.A.P.!

9

A LETTER FROM THE *OLD* ME TO THE *RE-FOUND* ME…

Hello, Nicole, it's nice to meet you again! I am so proud of you for putting yourself first for a whole year, while still progressing in your career, being a wife, and on top of that, blogging about it. I know that you made a lot of sacrifices, but you did it! It sounds like you have rediscovered the things that bring you joy as well as some new ones along the way. You have pretty much guaranteed that your kids are going to have a pretty well-adjusted mommy. I hope that you continue to stay committed to your self-care journey and bring some friends along the way. All moms need a little mommy break project in their lives.

Signed,

"Pre-Mommy" Nicole

Tear this out and post it on your vanity.

MOMMY BREAK MANIFESTO

I, _____, will be intentional about
(Your Name)

my self-care to ensure I am in the best physical,

mental, and emotional health to be the best

mommy I can be for my kids. I promise that I will

take a mommy break at least once per

(week/month), starting _____. I will not let
(Circle One)   *(Date)*

mommy guilt get in the way and will adopt a

Mommy Break by Any Means Necessary mindset. I

look forward to rediscovering the passions and

hobbies that make me a uniquely, awesome woman

(and mommy).

Signed: _____
(A Recommitted Mommy)